NEGOTIATION

Differences in opinion can be overcome if both sides are willing to listen to each other.

THE SCHOOL-TO-WORK LIBRARY

NEGOTIATION

Carolyn Simpson

GLOBE FEARON EDUCATIONAL PUBLISHER
A Division of Simon & Schuster
Upper Saddle River, New Jersey

Published in 1996 by The Rosen Publishing Group, Inc.
29 East 21st Street, New York, NY 10010

First Edition

Printed in the United States of America

ISBN 0-835-91766-5

Contents

Introduction

JAIME HAD A PROBLEM WITH SAM, HER SOCCER coach: She wasn't getting enough playing time. Other girls on the team got to play the whole four quarters, but Jaime always had to sit out one or two. She wasn't happy about the bench time.

At first Jaime wanted to quit the team. "That'll show the coach!" she thought. Of course, then she wouldn't be playing soccer at all.

Then she considered having her parents threaten the coach, but that might only make Sam mad at her.

Finally, Jaime remembered something her teacher had said about negotiating. Maybe this was a case she could negotiate. Good negotiating involved:

- defining the problem
- setting goals for yourself and guessing your opponent's goals
- presenting the facts
- listening to your opponent and thinking about his view

- considering this new information
- seeking a solution that will satisfy both of you

Jaime could easily state the problem: She wasn't getting to play all four quarters. So her goal was easy to define, too: She wanted to play a whole game. Putting herself in Sam's shoes was not so easy, though. If she were Sam, what would she want from the players?

"Sam likes to win games, so I guess he wants me to score goals. Maybe if I score some goals, he'll let me play longer," Jaime thought.

After the game, Jaime approached Sam.

"Coach," she said, "I'd like to play all four quarters in the next game. What do I need to do to get you to play me more?"

Sam thought for a minute. "Well, Jaime," he said, "if you didn't get so tired out there, I'd play you longer."

Jaime's face reddened. Was he telling her she was out of shape? She started to protest but then remembered what her teacher had said about listening. Give the other person the chance to say how he sees things. Listen closely and think over what he's said. Does this new information change your view of the problem?

As hard as it was to do, Jaime was determined to listen to Sam's comments. When Sam saw that

It is important to let someone know how you feel about an issue.

Jaime was indeed listening, he described what she could work on to improve her play.

After listening, Jaime said, "So, you're saying I need to practice running so I won't get so tired during games. I need to attack the ball and not be afraid of the other players getting in my way. And I need to kick harder."

"That's right, Jaime," Sam said. "If you do all those things, I can guarantee you'll be playing all four quarters."

Jaime wasn't mad at Sam anymore. Now she had a plan of action. She was going to run a mile every day and practice wind sprints. Maybe her sister could take her to the soccer fields to practice shooting during the week. If she practiced enough, she'd be the player her coach was looking for.

Sam was happy, too. He knew Jaime was angry about sitting on the bench, but now he knew she was willing to do something about it. Together they'd found a solution that made them both come out winners.

Negotiation is a way to do business with people to settle a common problem. You can either give in to other people's wishes or negotiate to find a better solution. Negotiating is a skill. You have to understand people in order to come up with good solutions. But learning to communicate these ideas is also a skill.

Negotiating can help you in all areas of your life, not just in sales or conflict management. Negotiating is part of secretarial jobs, management, and even clerical jobs. You use it in teaching, running a day-care center, social work, therapy, and administration. Politicians negotiate all the time, as do husbands and wives, parents and children.

Learning the right way to negotiate will make your life easier (and happier) in the long run. So why not get started right now?

Making your ideas known to others and listening to their views are often the first steps in resolving a conflict.

Negotiation in School

MS. MILLER WAS TEACHING A HUMAN RELATIONS class. Her students began to get uncomfortable when she brought up the topic of conflict.

"We don't have to do any confronting, do we?" Shelly asked.

"Well, of course you do," Ms. Miller said.

"Oh, no," another student groaned. "I can't stand conflict."

"What don't you like about it?" Ms. Miller asked.

"I don't like people getting all upset."

"But you're willing to be upset," Ms. Miller said.

"Well, it goes away eventually."

"What if I could show you how to negotiate so that you'd all come away satisfied, not upset?"

"Can't things get better without dragging everything into the open?"

"Not as a rule," Ms. Miller told them. "But relax. You learn to negotiate in steps. First, let's learn about people and work on our communication skills. Then we'll deal with the conflicts."

School offers many opportunities to practice communication skills.

So, with that thought in mind, let's look at classes you can take in high school to prepare yourself to be a better communicator.

English and Speech Classes
While you're in school, make the most of your English and speech courses. These courses prepare you to communicate. In order to negotiate, you have to know how to communicate well.

Communication involves four basic skills:

Reading
Writing

Speaking
Listening

You'll have mastered the first three skills if you do well in your English classes. Then all you have to worry about is your listening skills. It takes longer to develop those skills. You can train yourself to listen better by regularly listening to audiotapes. Try not to let your mind drift off when you're listening. You can also take the time to listen to someone with whom you don't agree. Think about her points and don't attempt to argue with her. Listening (without talking back) trains you to focus better. Thinking carefully about your opponent's point of view is an important part of negotiating.

Business Classes

Take business courses to learn about organizations and how companies work. Read all you can about successful managers; they're always good negotiators.

Psychology and Sociology Classes

Take these courses to learn more about people. Ninety to 95 percent of all communication is non-verbal. A wise negotiator learns how to read a person's body language: his gestures, his facial expressions, and especially his tone of voice. Words

Be aware of body language: It can show whether someone is confrontational or withdrawn.

form only a small part of communicating, and as you all know, people can lie. Body language is more believable.

Learn about group behavior. As a rule, people's positions become harder to change in groups. That's because they've publicly stated their positions and don't want to appear wishy-washy.

Learn how to practice "empathetic listening." Most people listen only to the first part of what people say; they're so busy thinking up their answer that they don't hear the rest. Empathetic listening requires you to stop reacting and simply listen. Try to stand in the other person's shoes and see things from her perspective.

History Classes and Current Events

Negotiating has gone on since the dawn of time. Because history has a way of repeating itself, you should study what negotiations were most successful. What lessons have we learned? The more you know about history and world events, the more you'll understand people.

Threat and aggression often lead to war. Bad negotiations often lead to more war. Look at what happened in Europe after World War I. The Allies humiliated Germany in their terms for peace. Because of this, many Germans welcomed the rise of Hitler, who promised to restore their pride.

What lessons are there still to learn? Look at all the violence in the world today. Could negotiating stop the conflicts?

Questions to Ask Yourself

There are many ways to practice negotiation skills in school. 1) Do you feel that you can communicate your ideas well through speech or writing? 2) What kinds of specialized classes or activities are offered at your school that can help to develop negotiation skills? 3) How has negotiation played a role in recent world affairs?

Opportunities to Negotiate

RONNIE RODE TO SCHOOL WITH HIS FATHER, WHO had to be at work by 7:30. That meant that Ronnie got to school well before the other students arrived. On most days he sat outside and finished his homework, but in the winter it was too cold to stand around. What he really wanted to do was go inside and get warm.

His father suggested a strategy.

The next day, Ronnie stopped by the principal's office. When he and the principal sat down to talk, Ronnie defined the problem. "Mr. Walker," he said, "every morning I get to school at 7:20 because that's when my father can drop me off. He can't change his work schedule. On most days, I sit outside and finish my homework, but it's getting too cold to do that now." (At this point, Ronnie has defined the problem from his perspective. Now he's going to state his goals.)

"What I'd like to be able to do is come inside at 7:20 on cold days and wait for school to start."

Negotiation skills can help you to hold your own when approaching an adult about a problem.

The principal frowned. "That's not possible," he said. "If I let you come inside, everyone else who comes early would want to do the same thing. Then we'd have a bunch of unsupervised students running around the building."

(Here Ronnie listened to his fellow negotiator's perspective and learned some new information. The principal's goal was not to leave any students unsupervised in the building.)

"Are you saying you don't mind my coming inside so early? You mind my being unsupervised?" Ronnie asked. (Here he is clarifying the problem from the other perspective.)

"That's correct," Mr. Walker said. "You can't get your father to bring you any later?" he asked, apparently checking whether there was another alternative.

"No, I'm afraid I can't. And it's a long walk. Too bad there isn't a bus I could take."

Suddenly Mr. Walker's eyes lit up. "That's it," he said.

"A bus?" Ronnie asked.

"Not a bus, but the room for the bus students," he said. "A lot of our bus students come early, so they go to the bus room. There's always a teacher to watch them. If you have to come early, you can do what the bus students do."

"So I can come inside?" Ronnie said.

A successful negotiation satisfies both parties.

"In bad weather, you can come in with the bus students," Mr. Walker said. "How does that sound to you?"

"It's fine by me," Ronnie said. "I can use another study hall."

In any good negotiation, the outcome should satisfy both parties. In this example, Ronnie got to go inside, which was his goal, and Mr. Walker saw to it that Ronnie was supervised, which was his goal. Everyone went away happy.

Opportunities to negotiate are everywhere. You might have to work out differences with teachers (over your classroom behavior or grades). When you negotiate with authority figures, you may not always get what you want because authority figures have the power to make certain rules. Still, it's worth trying when you have a conflict.

Schools are changing to match the work environment. Now that people are working in teams and committees on the job, schools are encouraging students to develop group projects in the classroom. Working with others fosters cooperation and better decision-making. On the other hand, whenever people get together, there's bound to be conflict because people have different ways of looking at things and getting things done. Group efforts require good communication and negotiating skills.

Three students were asked to put together a bulletin board for the school's front office. Susan, Donna, and Carla got together during a study hall.

"I've given this a lot of thought," Susan said. "We should make a winter scene, maybe some snowmen or something. I'm good at making snowmen."

"What about the purpose of the bulletin board? Aren't we supposed to be saying something about the school?" Carla asked.

"Sure, sure," Susan said. "You can do the wording if you want."

In group projects, group members may overlook the needs and goals of others in the group.

"I don't want to do the words. I can't write letters. How about if you do the lettering, Donna? You're good at that."

"Well, sure, I can do the lettering, but I can draw other stuff, too."

"There isn't anything else to draw. I'll do one of the snowmen and you do the other, Carla," Susan said. "Oh, you can do some background, Donna, but not much. We don't want it to interfere with the focal point."

Donna looked unhappy. Susan and Carla set to work right away, drawing and cutting out two huge snowmen. Donna put up the white background paper and started cutting out letters. Having had no say in the design, she didn't really care how it all turned out anyway. She'd already lost interest in the project.

Group projects always turn out badly, she thought. I get stuck doing the stuff no one else wants to do.

If you were Donna, would you have given in so easily? This was a good occasion to practice negotiating. Right from the start, Donna should have jumped in and helped define the problem. *What were they supposed to be designing?* She also needed to think out her own goals. *I'd like to do some drawing, not just the lettering.* Then they all could have put forth their ideas. As it turned out, Susan threw out the idea and decided how it would be carried out. That wasn't negotiating; that was dictating.

Let's look at the negotiating skills you need to problem-solve with people.

1. You need to define the problem. What exactly is the problem and what needs to happen to fix it? Who is involved in the solution (because that's the person with whom you should be negotiating)?
2. Before you talk to the person with whom you have the problem, role-play what you're going to

All group members should participate in decision-making.

say. Practice saying it to a friend. Your friend can pretend to be mad, sorry, or uninterested so that you learn how to handle any reaction.

3. Be straightforward but tactful with your fellow negotiator.

4. Once you've defined the problem, let the other person give you his or her perspective. Listen, and try to see his or her viewpoint. This is called perspective-taking.

5. Watch your tone of voice. Often, it's not so much *what* you say as *how* you say it. Don't be nasty or sarcastic.

6. Be fair as you both seek a solution. Be flexible, too.

7. In many negotiations, you're going to want to keep the relationship. That's why it's important to search for a solution that works for everyone.

8. If you discover you're part of the problem, admit it and apologize.

Questions to Ask Yourself

Opportunities for negotiation can be found in many aspects of your life. 1) How do you normally handle the situation when you disagree with a parent, friend, or sibling? 2) Have you considered how others might view a situation entirely differently from the way you view it? 3) Do you work well with other people in group projects?

Learning Negotiation Through Extracurricular Activities

WHEN KYLA WAS PRESIDENT OF HER 4-H CLUB, she learned that it is not always easy to lead. That spring, some older members had decided that they wanted to run their meetings without any parents present. Kyla's father was the parent-leader, and he didn't go along with the idea. That presented a problem to Kyla. If she went along with her fellow members, she'd be going against her father's wishes. If she went along with her father, she'd be going against her friends' wishes.

Here was an opportunity to practice good negotiation skills. Kyla could have asked the parents and the kids to get together and discuss the problem and to find a solution to suit everybody. The parents could have asked the kids why they wanted meetings without parents present. The kids could have given reasons for their suggestion. Once the needs

Sports team members have many opportunities to negotiate—with teammates, coaches, referees, and other teams.

(or issues) were out in the open, the solution might have presented itself.

But there was no negotiating. The parents refused to allow the meetings if they were barred from attending. No parents, no meetings. The kids lost. (But so did the parents, because their children were angry with them for a long time afterward.)

Groups are good opportunities to practice negotiating with others. Whenever two or more people get together, you've got different interests and agendas.

It takes skill to find the common ground within these different agendas.

You also learn to negotiate when you play sports. You negotiate your way onto the team; you negotiate your playing time (as Jaime had to do with Sam), and you negotiate your relationship with others.

During a soccer match, Jenny was running for the ball and accidentally kicked another player in the shins. The player went down.

Fran, Jenny's teammate, came running over and hissed, "That was a cheap shot! What'd you kick her for?"

Jenny's face reddened. "You think I did that on purpose? Come on, it was an accident."

Fran strode off; the player got up and the game continued. Jenny couldn't help but keep replaying Fran's remark. She got madder and madder because everyone else on the field probably heard it, too. Suddenly, the ball came whizzing by Jenny, and she missed the shot. Her coach took her out to calm down.

Sitting on the bench gave Jenny time to think about how she should deal with Fran. (Fran was the coach's daughter, so it wasn't going to be easy.) Jenny defined the problem: a rude remark made where others could hear it.

She knew what she wanted to have happen in the future: no more rude remarks. She tried to put herself in Fran's shoes. Maybe Fran really thought Jenny had kicked that girl on purpose. Well, if she really thought that, she must have felt she should say something.

The game was over, and Fran ran over to grab a water bottle. Jenny handed her the bottle. "Fran," she said, "I want you to know I didn't kick that girl on purpose."

"Well, it's not like you to do that," Fran said, "but it looked that way. No big deal; we won the game."

"It's a big deal to me," Jenny said. "Everyone heard you say that."

"Oh, I'm sorry if that embarrassed you," Fran said.

"Thanks," Jenny said (acknowledging the apology).

(She could have let the subject go, but the negotiation wasn't complete. After all, Jenny didn't want these remarks to continue. She wanted Fran to understand how she felt about what had happened.)

"Fran, it's really distracting to hear you yell something when I'm trying to play. I don't mind what you have to say; I just don't want to hear it during the game."

Fran wiped her face. "I didn't mean anything by

it," she said. "You played a good game. I'm sorry I messed you up."

For the first time, Jenny felt better about her relationship with Fran. She'd asserted herself, and Fran had listened to her and understood. The solution, saving any comments until after the game, would work for both of them.

It's wise to practice negotiating when the stakes are low. You don't want to make a negotiation out of everything in your life, but it's useful to practice before you have to negotiate some of the bigger things in life. In that way you will be better prepared to deal with more demanding challenges in an effective manner.

Think about some of the conflicts you might be having with a classmate or a teammate. Define the problems, as Jenny did. Decide how you might deal with them without attacking your opponent. Then practice what you might say ahead of time.

When you're ready to negotiate, you should be prepared for anything. Be ready for surprises, but expect fairness. We often get exactly what we're looking for.

Once you get in the habit of seeking good solutions, you'll probably start seeing conflict as a challenge, not an ordeal.

Questions to Ask Yourself

Because they almost always involve interaction with others, extracurricular activities can help you to develop good negotiation skills. 1) What kind of extracurricular activities are you involved in? 2) How might you approach a negotiation with your adviser or principal if a group you are involved in wants to go on a field trip? 3) Do you feel that you are able to make yourself heard in a group of people?

Learning to Negotiate on the Job

MERCI HAD JUST WON TICKETS TO A CONCERT.
There was only one problem—she was supposed to
work that Friday. She called her boss to beg for the
evening off, but he reminded her that the restaurant
was already short-staffed. He couldn't afford to let
her off.

Merci thought about quitting. This concert was
more important than any waitressing job. She could
always get another job. (But would any other job be
as good? And did she really want to start filling out
applications all over again?)

Then she had a better idea. Maybe someone else
could work in her place. Didn't Abby have Fridays
off?

Before Merci picked up the phone, she considered the problem some more. In order to negotiate
with someone, you need to know what her goals
are. That way you can try to satisfy them as well as
your own. She knew that Abby needed money because she'd just bought a car, and tips on Friday

On the job, you may need to negotiate a schedule change or job assignment with a coworker.

nights were always good. She checked the schedule and saw that Abby was supposed to work on Sunday (a day when tips weren't very good).

Armed with this information, Merci dialed Abby.

"I just won tickets to a concert for this Friday night, Abby, but I can't get off work. I wondered if you'd fill in for me."

Merci heard Abby's sigh. "Merci, I haven't had a Friday night off in a long time."

"I know," Merci replied, "but I wouldn't ask if it weren't really important. I'm willing to make it worth your while."

"How's that?" asked Abby.

"Well, if you take my Friday night, you'll be making a lot in tips. Better than you'd make this Sunday. I'll trade you Friday for Sunday. You'll still get a day off this weekend, and you will make more money than you would have."

"Well, I am pressed for cash," Abby said.

"Then, is it a deal?" Merci asked.

"Oh, okay," Abby said. "Maybe I'll need a favor in the future."

Working a part-time job gives you a lot of opportunities to negotiate. As in the above example, you might want to trade days off. That often calls for patience, creativity, and fair play.

At some point, you'll start thinking about a raise. Do you know how to negotiate a good one?

Let's go back to that list of negotiating skills. First, define the problem. The problem isn't that *you need a raise*. That's your *position*. You think a raise will solve your problem. The problem might be: *"Everyone else got a raise, so I want one too,"* or *"I deserve more money for all that I'm supposed to do,"* or *"I'm broke half the time; I think I'd better start making more money."*

Now, reflecting on the problem, what do I need? More money for the things I'm already doing? More opportunities to earn money? Or do I really need some form of recognition that I've been doing a good job all this time?

If you decide you really need more money for the things that you're doing, think of a fair amount to ask for. Aim high (but not ridiculously high). Some employers like to haggle over amounts; they'll always offer a lower amount than you request. If you have to haggle, you might as well start higher than you need.

Make sure you know a realistic amount. Find out what others are making for the same type of work. (That's called doing your research.)

Remember the goals of your fellow negotiator, though. If an offer seems fair, he or she is more apt to take it. If you want a raise, make sure you can show why you deserve one. If your employer just doesn't have the money to give you a raise, consider other benefits. If you work in a store, could she offer you a better discount? Could she offer incentives for increasing sales? (If you helped get more business, she'd have more money. Right?) Never come up with only one solution. Have several "fallback positions," which are plans in case your first offer doesn't work out.

So far, you've defined your needs (and considered the needs of your opponent). You've stated your "facts" and listened to hers. You've tried to think up a solution that will meet both your needs, but all she has said is, "Let me think about it."

Give your employer time to make her decision. Sometimes she'll make the decision right there on the spot. Other times she may want to check her books to see if it will work out for her. Don't push for a quick decision. Most people don't react well to being pushed. Set a realistic deadline for the decision to be made, and don't bring the subject up in the meantime.

Always develop your *best alternative to a negotiated agreement*, called a BATNA. If your offer is rejected, what is your best alternative? Quitting? If your BATNA is a good one (you have another job offer), you're in a better position to negotiate with your boss.

There's more to negotiate than wages. Some

You may be able to negotiate something you have, such as computer skills, to get something you want.

people trade services for something they want.

Mark wanted to take tae kwon do lessons, but the lessons turned out to be more costly than his parents could afford. He decided to approach the owner and suggest ways he could "work off" the lessons.

The owner was struggling with his computer. "You don't happen to know someone who can fix computers, do you?" he asked Mark.

"What's the problem?" Mark asked. "I know a little about computers. We've got the same brand at home."

The first step in dealing with a difficult customer is to determine why he or she is upset.

"Really?" the owner said, looking Mark over. "Think you know why this keeps shutting down?" he asked, moving over to give Mark some room.

After Mark identified the computer's problem, he thought about the tae kwon do lessons. He already knew his goal: get some lessons. Now he knew the owner's goals: get some help with his office work. Why couldn't he offer to work in the office part time in exchange for tae kwon do lessons? It wouldn't hurt to ask.

When Dealing with Difficult People

Negotiating seems easy when you're dealing with people who sincerely want to make a deal (or settle a problem). It's harder when people don't want to change or don't want to listen to you. That, however, is when you most need all your skills.

If you're dealing with a difficult person (an unhappy customer or an uncooperative coworker), pay more attention to body language and tone of voice. However, you should still use the same skills.

1. Someone needs to define the problem. If the customer is just rambling on about the poor service or the product, try to put his anger into words. If he can't tell you exactly what's bothering him, make a good guess and ask if that sounds right.

2. Obviously, a goal for you is to calm the customer. You'll probably succeed in this if you can figure out what the customer wants. (And what he wants is not always what he says. Maybe he just wants someone to listen to him.)
3. Listen to the difficult person. Don't try to argue with him. Sometimes people just need to let off steam. Once they've ranted and raved, they'll settle down on their own.
4. Reflect on what he has said. Is your company at fault? Are you at fault? What can be done to fix the situation?
5. When someone is angry and yelling, don't get caught up in the emotional display. Lower your voice and be calm. If he wants to hear you, he'll have to quiet down (which is what you want).
6. When you've heard the facts (yours and his), try to clarify the situation (or problem). Make sure you both understand the problem.
7. Propose solutions, but be willing to compromise. Nobody ever said the winner is the one who comes up with the solution. The solution should make everyone a winner.

Questions to Ask Yourself

Your opinions on the job may differ from those of your employer, coworkers, or customers. It is important to learn to work through differences of opinion so that you can accomplish your tasks effectively. 1) Do you feel that you fully understand what your boss expects of you? 2) Do you ever disagree with your boss or with a coworker about how a certain job should be done? 3) What is a BATNA, and how can you use it effectively when negotiating?

The Abundance Mentality

THERE ARE TWO KINDS OF PEOPLE IN THIS WORLD: those who believe in the "abundance mentality" and those who believe in the "scarcity mentality." If you believe in the abundance mentality, you're not worried about beating your opponent because you know there are enough rewards to go around. You're concerned about finding solutions that will satisfy both of you. If he's happy with the outcome, and you're happy with the outcome, you'll both work hard to honor your agreement.

However, if you believe in the "scarcity mentality," you can't let your opponent win anything. That's because you're sure there's not enough to cover both your needs. Anything he gets, you haven't gotten.

Rhonda has a summer job as a telemarketer. She has a list of people to call each day. Her job is to call them and try to sell them her company's product, a set of books about gardening. Some people just hang up on her. Some people, gardening enthusiasts, are interested right away. Most people are interested enough to stay on the phone but they need convincing from Rhonda. She uses negotiation skills to make a sale. One day, one of her calls went like this:

Customer: Hello?

Rhonda: Hello, my name is Rhonda and I'm calling from the Bountiful Gardens Book Company. I'd like to talk with you about a great new set of gardening books we're offering for just $34.95.

Customer: I don't usually like to order things over the phone. I need to see them first.

Rhonda: Well, with our product we have an excellent return policy. Just call us if you aren't satisfied, and we'll have the books picked up free.

Customer: I'm . . . Well, I'm not much of a gardener.

Rhonda: That's why these books may be perfect for you. They go from simple to advanced. The first book is for people who've never gardened before. Then, as your gardening skills improve, you move through the series. The last book has some very advanced techniques.

Customer: Well, I don't have much of a yard anyway.

Rhonda: No problem! There are chapters on gardening for small yards and indoor gardening, too.

Customer: I don't know. I've just never been very interested in gardening.

Rhonda: We're confident that these books will get you excited about it. Think about eating a salad with greens and tomatoes that you've grown yourself! Or giving someone a bouquet of flowers from your own garden.

Customer: I guess that would be nice. But it just takes too much time.

Rhonda: Not with these techniques. They take no time at all, especially with the full-color photos illustrating each step.

Customer: OK, I guess I could try them out.

Rhonda: Great! You won't be disappointed.

In this negotiation, Rhonda represented her product honestly and provided the customer with the information he needed. She adjusted quickly to new facts and ideas the customer presented. She listened to what the customer was saying and presented new facts about her product that were appropriate to the customer's concerns. Using effective communication skills, Rhonda demonstrated how the product would meet the customer's needs. Rhonda was also practicing abundance mentality. She had the mindset that both she and her customer would gain if she made a sale. The customer was worried about getting a bad deal or being "ripped off." Rhonda was able to convince the customer that he would gain something in the deal.

You may have to negotiate with your boss or a colleague before your ideas are implemented.

Alan was a computer software salesman at a company where he had worked part time while he was in high school. He had spent months working to negotiate a sale with a large company. He got the owners to tell him what they wanted (their goals) so that he could match that to his goal (making a profit). When it came down to the final offer, it looked as if he was not going to make a sale. The company said that it couldn't pay any more than $200,000. Alan couldn't sell the software for less than $300,000. Was the deal off?

Alan realized that his BATNA was no sale at all. He was going to have to use his negotiation skills.

Alan sat down with the owners and attacked the problem: how to get as much software as they could for $200,000. Alan suggested a payment plan by which they could buy some of the software now and buy more as more money became available, as well as different equipment. In the end, he got the sale, made his profit, and gave the company a good deal in the process. Everyone went away happy.

No matter what you do in your life, you'll always have reason to negotiate. When you buy a house, you negotiate with the seller (and maybe even the bank).

When you buy a car, you have to negotiate. Do your research so you'll be in the best position to bargain. Check prices and deals at various car dealerships. Based on what is available, decide what you want to pay. If you negotiate a deal that's good for both of you, you'll be able to continue the relationship. If you focus on outwitting the dealer, you'll damage the relationship. (Who cares about keeping a relationship with a car salesman? That depends on where you want to get your car serviced later.)

Every job requires negotiating skills. Where there are people, there will be conflict. Increasingly, the workplace is organized around teams and groups, so you'll be thrown together with a variety of people to accomplish a task.

Some people actually specialize in solving disputes. Organizations hire employee relations coordinators (to settle company in-fighting); labor unions hire mediators and negotiators to settle strikes. The police department even hires special negotiators to work with them in hostage situations.

The successful negotiator is both a good communicator and a good listener. These are skills that will help in keeping any job.

Questions to Ask Yourself

Abundance mentality refers to the belief that there are rewards for everyone, even in a situation of conflict or disagreement. It can help you to work with others to achieve a compromise. 1) Do you tend to believe in the abundance mentality, or scarcity mentality (the belief that there is not enough for everyone)? 2) How might you sell a drab-looking but fuel-efficient used car to a skeptical customer? 3) How might abundance mentality be useful in negotiating with your boss for a raise?

Strategies of Principled Negotiating

PRINCIPLED NEGOTIATING GROWS OUT OF AN abundance mentality. The negotiator focuses on *issues*, not the *people behind them*. He doesn't take a position and hold on for dear life. Doing that limits your solutions to a problem. There's always more than one solution, so keep your options open. The essence of principled negotiating is this: If you play fairly and seek to satisfy *everyone's* goals, you'll all be winners. And winners keep to their agreements.

Specific Strategies

1. Know what you want out of the negotiation, and know what you can afford to give up to get it. This is called bargaining, giving something up to get something you want more. Most people are willing to give up some of the smaller stuff.

2. Knowing what you want means having done your homework. Never go into a negotiation unprepared. Be sure you have all the numbers (and facts) to back up what you say.

Your arguments will be more convincing if you have facts to back them up.

3. Understand your opponent. That means researching him beforehand so you know where he stands with his company. (If you're looking to buy a car, know what kind of dealership you're negotiating with.)

4. Watch your opponent's body language. If someone is nervous, he'll be making a lot of nervous gestures: jiggling his foot, tapping his pen on the table. If he's deceiving you, he may not look you in the eye. Observe your opponent carefully to see if his gestures match what he's saying.

5. Ask open-ended questions (questions that require more than a yes or no answer). Find out his issues and values. The more issues that are out on the table, the more you have to bargain over.

6. "Unpack" *all* the issues related to the problem. You don't want last-minute surprises just when you think you've reached agreement. When you think you have them all out in the open, read them back to your opponent. "Let's see, you're concerned about fast delivery of our product, good quality, and continued service. Is there anything else?"

7. Be patient as you consider all the issues. Negotiations take time. The person who is eager for a quick solution is likely to jump at the first offer, which is rarely the best solution. If your opponent makes an offer, don't accept it on the

spot. Slow down and think the matter over. You might even want to take a break to consider it.

8. Know the power of silence. Don't rush in to fill up the quiet. Americans, in general, are nervous with silence; they end up babbling if it goes on too long. You can learn a lot about your opponent if he's nervous with silence and you're not. He's going to tell you more than he means to.

9. Brainstorm with your opponent; don't consider him an enemy. Come up with many solutions even if they don't seem practical at first. The point is to get in the habit of thinking creatively. You might even brainstorm solutions with your friends before your negotiation takes place.

A list of DON'Ts

1. Don't be dishonest. You can be evasive if you need to keep some information to yourself; just don't lie. It destroys trust.

2. Don't be hostile or sarcastic to get your way.

3. Don't threaten your opponent (unless you fully intend to carry through on your threat). However, threats can backfire. Some people won't want to deal with you if you threaten them.

4. Don't get hung up thinking someone is more powerful than you. We all have power. It's one of those things that's in the eye of the beholder.

You'll get a better deal if you see yourself as strong.

5. Don't let your opponent wear you down. If you're getting tired, take a break. The wise negotiator knows his limits. You start giving away too much when you're tired.

6. Don't lose sight of the relationship. You don't want to win the deal and lose the customer. That's why it's so important not to play dirty tricks to win.

When Your Opponent Plays Dirty . . .

Let's say, for example, that you are negotiating with your boss for an increase in your hourly wage. She tells you to come by at around 3 P.M., but she's not there. The next day she says she's busy all week. She may be playing dirty. There are other ways of playing dirty.

1. If your opponent becomes aggressive (shakes his finger in your face, threatens you, calls you names), don't react. Often, it's a trick to make you nervous so you'll give him what he wants. Focus on "the issue," not the person creating the scene. (If aggressive behavior makes you nervous, role-play with a friend beforehand so you won't panic.) Keeping your sense of humor will help you relax.

2. If the setting for your negotiation is uncomfort-

able (a hard chair, the sun in your eyes, or the room too cold), understand that your opponent may have done this on purpose. Ask for a different chair. Ask him to pull down the shade or turn off the air conditioner. Usually an opponent will stop manipulating your environment if he knows you're on to him.

3. Some opponents use the good guy/bad guy approach. One will be nasty with you while the other will try to win you over. Ask if they're using the good guy/bad guy routine. Bringing the subject into the open usually makes them stop.

4. If your opponent keeps dragging out your negotiation sessions and refuses to come to a decision, set a deadline. Some people try to wear you down with delays.

5. If your opponent wants to change the rules after you've agreed to them (by trying to get you to concede on things you thought you'd already settled), remind him of the terms and the rules. People will get away with only as much as you let them.

6. In the end, if you keep focusing on the issues, not the people, you may be able to turn your opponent toward more principled negotiating.

Two last things. Once you've agreed to terms (even on single issues), get everything in writing.

Then summarize what you've agreed to (especially if you're stuck on any issue). It helps to see how much you *have* been able to resolve when you think you're not getting anywhere.

(This is what Alan did to negotiate his sale of computer software. When they locked horns on the price, Alan went back over a list of things they had agreed to: a good product, quick servicing, and a promise to buy back items they weren't happy with. Realizing how much they had to lose, both parties were more willing to brainstorm other ways to make the deal.)

However, if you simply can't find a solution that serves you both, maybe this is a deal you can't make at this point in time. No deal is often better than an unfair one.

Questions to Ask Yourself

Principled negotiating helps you to keep the real goal of the negotiation in mind: resolving the issue, not cutting down the other person. 1) What is an issue about which you feel strongly? 2) How can body language play an important role in a negotiation? 3) How would you handle a situation where your negotiating partner "plays dirty"?

Being able to work well with others will become even more important in the workplace of the future.

Negotiation and Your Career

INTERNATIONAL COMPETITION HAS FORCED NORTH
America to rethink its workplace. Today, many
companies are striving to achieve the high-
performance workplace. In the high-performance
workplace, the structure is often decentralized,
meaning that people work as peers rather than in
relationships of power over one another. Employees
are encouraged and empowered to make their own
decisions. They are often organized into work
teams. But what happens when people are working
together as teams to make decisions and carry out
the same tasks? They won't always agree on the
decisions to be made or on how the work should be
done. That's why negotiation skills are more important than ever. In the workplace of the future, your
boss probably won't be telling you what to do all
the time. You'll have to negotiate with your boss
about the things to be done; you'll have to negotiate
with your team to get those things done.

Most companies rely on employees to make decisions and accomplish tasks in teams.

Joel is an intern at an advertising agency. He thinks advertising is something he may want to do someday. He sees the process of negotiation at work. He knows that the head of the agency first meets with a client to discuss the type of ad campaign the client would like. The client presents the company's product and points out the qualities of the product that they would like the ad to highlight. The head of the agency takes this information to the creative department. The art team comes up with a visual design. The writing team writes the ad. The creative department must work together, of course, and agree on a concept so that the writing and the design go together. When they've come up with the ad, they take it back to the company president, who decides whether it fits with what the client has described. The creative team may have to negotiate and explain why they came up with that particular ad. They may have to make changes in the ad. When they and the company president agree on the ad, the president presents it to the client. The creative team may be called in to negotiate any changes with the client. They may have to present evidence and arguments for why the ad will work.

"I've seen how important negotiation is," says Joel. "The first priority is to satisfy the client, but sometimes the client needs to be convinced that our ad campaign will really sell the product. We may have to get the client to change his original vision. We have to be willing to change some things, too. In the end, everyone's had to compromise, but they're satisfied with the final result."

This is the type of negotiation that goes on in the workplace. Negotiation is one of the most important skills employees can have. If people can't agree, things don't get done. Negotiation is one of the most critical skills you'll need for getting along with people and for achieving the things you want to achieve. As you think about your future career, think about how negotiation is a part of that career. It will always figure in somehow. It's best to be prepared.

The skills you learned in this book will help you to work more effectively with your future bosses and coworkers. If problems arise, you'll know how to use "I" statements and practice empathetic listening. Your negotiating skills will make you stand out—whether you're negotiating multimillion-dollar deals or negotiating for a better airfare for your boss's business trip. Practicing negotiation now, with friends, family, and teachers, can pave the way for your future negotiations in the world of work.

Questions to Ask Yourself

The high-performance workplace emphasizes cooperation and teamwork between coworkers. 1) Does your current job offer opportunities to practice working with others? 2) What is your long-term job or career goal? 3) How might the need to negotiate arise in this field?

Glossary

abundance mentality The belief that there are enough resources for everyone.

adversary Your opponent (otherwise known as your negotiating partner).

BATNA Best alternative to a negotiated agreement.

brainstorming Coming up with ideas.

concede To give up something in order to get something you want more.

conflict resolution Solution of a problem that was causing conflict.

empathetic listening Listening in order to understand the other person and his perspective.

fallback position Your position, should your first choice not be accepted.

hardball negotiating Taking an aggressive approach to negotiating.

interest bargaining Bargaining on the issues, not people's positions.

manipulating Getting a person to do something, usually through trickery.

negotiate To do business with someone to solve a mutual problem.

open-ended questions Questions that call for more than a yes or no answer.

positional bargaining Taking a position in a negotiation and arguing for it.

strategy An overall plan of action.

tactic A maneuver to achieve the plan.

unpacking Determining all your opponent's issues or complaints.

For Further Reading

Bazerman, Max. *Negotiating Rationally*. New York: The Free Press, 1992.

Carter, Jimmy. *Talking Peace*. New York: Dutton Children's Books, 1993.

Dolan, John Patrick. *Negotiate Like the Pros*. New York: Putnam Publishing Group, 1992.

Fisher, Roger, and Ury, William. *Getting to Yes*. New York: Penguin Books, 1983.

Freund, James C. *Smart Negotiating*. New York: Simon & Schuster, 1992.

Karrass, Chester. *The Negotiating Game*. New York: HarperCollins Publishers, 1994.

Kennedy, Gavin. *The Perfect Negotiator*. New York: Wings Books, 1992.

Pollan, Stephen, and Levine, Mark. *The Total Negotiator*. New York: Avon Books, 1994.

Schapiro, Nicole. *Negotiating for Your Life*. New York: Henry Holt and Co., 1993.

Index

About the Author

Carolyn Simpson teaches Psychology and Human Relations at Tulsa Junior College in Tulsa, Oklahoma. She is currently designing a course to teach on interpersonal conflict.

Photos

Katherine Hsu

Layout and Design

Kim Sonsky

Acknowledgments

Many thanks to Lee Clarke for his tips on negotiating sales agreements.